US MILITARY EQUIPMENT
AND VEHICLES

US NAVY
EQUIPMENT AND VEHICLES

BY DOUGLAS HUSTAD

CONTENT CONSULTANT
STEPHEN K. STEIN, PhD
ASSOCIATE PROFESSOR OF HISTORY
UNIVERSITY OF MEMPHIS

Kids Core
An Imprint of Abdo Publishing
abdobooks.com

abdobooks.com

Published by Abdo Publishing, a division of ABDO, PO Box 398166, Minneapolis, Minnesota 55439. Copyright © 2022 by Abdo Consulting Group, Inc. International copyrights reserved in all countries. No part of this book may be reproduced in any form without written permission from the publisher. Kids Core™ is a trademark and logo of Abdo Publishing.

Printed in the United States of America, North Mankato, Minnesota
052021
092021

Cover Photo: Mass Communication Specialist 2nd Class Paul L. Archer/US Navy
Interior Photos: Mass Communication Specialist 2nd Class D'Andre L. Roden/US Navy, 4–5; Shutterstock Images, 6; Mass Communication Specialist 2nd Class Kris R. Lindstrom/US Navy, 8; Mass Communication Specialist 3rd Class Matthew Jackson/Defense Visual Information Distribution Service, 10–11; Mass Communication Specialist 2nd Class Taylor DiMartino/US Navy, 12, 14; Mass Communication Specialist 3rd Class Karolina A. Oseguera/Defense Visual Information Distribution Service, 15; Chief Mass Communication Specialist Jayme Pastoric/US Navy, 16; Mass Communication Specialist 1st Class Michael D. Cole/US Navy, 18–19; Mass Communication Specialist 3rd Class Nicholas V. Huynh/US Navy, 21; Mass Communication Specialist 1st Class Amanda R. Gray/US Navy, 23; Mass Communication Specialist 1st Class Joshua D. Sheppard/Defense Visual Information Distribution Service, 24; Mass Communication Specialist 3rd Class Sean Castellano/US Navy, 26; Mass Communication Specialist 1st Class Jason C. Swink/US Navy, 28; Erik Hildebrandt/US Navy, 29 (top); Lt. Ed Early/US Navy, 29 (bottom)

Editor: Katharine Hale
Series Designer: Jake Nordby

Library of Congress Control Number: 2020948335

Publisher's Cataloging-in-Publication Data

Names: Hustad, Douglas, author.
Title: US Navy equipment and vehicles / by Douglas Hustad
Description: Minneapolis, Minnesota : Abdo Publishing, 2022 | Series: US military equipment and vehicles | Includes online resources and index.
Identifiers: ISBN 9781532195471 (lib. bdg.) | ISBN 9781644946206 (pbk.) | ISBN 9781098215781 (ebook)
Subjects: LCSH: Navies--Juvenile literature. | Sea-power--Juvenile literature. | Coastal surveillance--Juvenile literature. | Vehicles, Military--Juvenile literature. | Military supplies--Juvenile literature. | Military paraphernalia--Juvenile literature.
Classification: DDC 623.7--dc23

CONTENTS

As of 2020, the US Navy had 11 active aircraft carriers. This is more than any other country.

A CITY AT SEA

Out in the middle of the ocean, there is a city of thousands. It cuts through the water at almost 35 miles per hour (56 km/h). On top, there is an airport. Hundreds of people move planes and helicopters across a deck the length of three football fields.

Carrier Catapults

Each aircraft carrier has four catapults to launch aircraft. But it can only use two at once. Aircraft land on the diagonal runway.

This is no ordinary ship. This is a US aircraft carrier. A carrier deck is a busy place. Hundreds of sailors work different jobs. One guides an aircraft to the runway. Another sets up the **catapult** that will launch the plane into the air.

The catapult holds the aircraft's front wheel. Then it launches the plane to takeoff speed. The pilot will go from zero to 150 miles per hour (240 km/h) in two seconds.

The pilot gives a salute to show she's ready. A catapult officer salutes back. The plane rockets into the air in the blink of an eye.

Ford Class

A new class of aircraft carrier was launched with the USS *Gerald R. Ford* in 2017. It was the first newly-designed US carrier in 40 years. The *Ford* is the largest active aircraft carrier in the world. It was named after the United States' thirty-eighth president.

Catapult officers on aircraft carriers wear yellow shirts.

About the Navy

The US Navy is a branch of the US military. Its mission is to protect the United States at sea.

It has many sailors, ships, and weapons. A carrier and its aircraft are just one form of defense. Each ship has its own weapons to defend itself.

The navy is known for its power at sea. But it has a wide range of other equipment and vehicles. They all help the navy keep the United States safe.

Explore Online

Visit the website below. Does the video give any new information on aircraft carriers that wasn't in Chapter One?

Testing Ford's New Catapults

abdocorelibrary.com/navy-equipment-vehicles

Navy sailors can monitor
weapons using computers
inside ships.

NAVY WEAPONS

Navy weapons are controlled by the Aegis Weapon System (AWS). The AWS is not a weapon itself. It is a system of computer technology to guide weapons throughout an attack. It has **radar** to detect a threat. It can track an enemy plane or ship.

The USS *Curtis Wilbur* launched a Tomahawk missile during a demonstration in 2019.

Then it gives the crew options of what weapons to launch. AWS is on board every navy ship.

Navy ships carry missiles. Missiles are rockets that carry explosives. These rockets have computer systems that guide them to their targets.

The Tomahawk is a common navy missile. It was first used in 1991. Tomahawks can fly up to 1,000 miles (1,600 km). They travel at 550 miles per hour (885 km/h). Tomahawk missiles fly very low and fast. It's hard to see them coming. That makes them hard to shoot down.

The USS *Midway* Museum

The carrier USS *Midway* served from 1945 to 1992. In 2004, it became a museum in San Diego, California. *Midway* is the largest carrier on display in the world. Visitors can get a behind-the-scenes look at life on a carrier. This includes essentials such as a barber shop and laundry.

Sailors work together to load an MK 46 torpedo into a tube for firing.

A missile that travels underwater is called a torpedo. Navy submarines launch torpedoes. Submarines spend most of their time underwater. That is where they launch attacks.

Man the Guns

Navy ships also carry big guns. Guns are usually used to attack enemy ships that get too close. These guns are very powerful

The MK 110 57mm is one type of gun used on navy ships.

and fast. They launch hundreds of rounds per minute. They are not as effective for long-range attacks.

The navy uses mine countermeasure devices to help find and deactivate enemy mines.

One unpowered weapon the navy uses is the mine. Mines are among the oldest navy weapons. They were first used in the Revolutionary War (1775–83). Mines do not travel to their targets. Mines are dropped in the water to wait for an enemy ship. When the ship gets too close, the mine explodes. Mines protect an area without sailors having to be nearby. This keeps sailors safe. Mines are just another weapon in the navy's huge **arsenal**.

Further Evidence

Look at the website below. Does it give any new evidence to support Chapter Two?

Tomahawk Cruise Missile

abdocorelibrary.com/navy-equipment
-vehicles

Carrier strike groups vary
in the number and types of
ships involved.

CHAPTER 3

THE FLEET

The US Navy's **fleet** is huge. The navy has about 300 warships. They come in all shapes and sizes. They have different jobs and abilities.

US carriers are powered by **nuclear reactors**. Nuclear fuel lasts a long time.

Carriers can go 20 years without refueling. The navy has other nuclear-powered ships too.

The carrier is the main ship in a Carrier Strike Group (CSG). A CSG is the most powerful attack group the navy has. It involves a carrier and six to ten other ships. There are also 65 to 70 aircraft. A CSG includes 7,500 sailors.

Cruisers and Destroyers

A CSG always includes one cruiser. Cruisers are the second-largest ship in the navy fleet. They carry missiles. A cruiser is able to attack almost any kind of target with missiles. Cruisers are about half the length of a carrier. They have crews of more than 300 people. Cruisers can also carry two helicopters.

The USS *Bunker Hill, right,* is a cruiser. The USS *Barry, left,* is a destroyer.

Destroyers are another part of a CSG. The navy has more destroyers than any other kind of ship. Destroyers are shorter and faster than cruisers. Destroyers protect bigger ships.

They carry missiles that can attack targets on land, in the sea, or in the air.

Under the Sea

A navy submarine is unlike any other ship. Submarines travel hundreds of feet below the surface of the ocean. They can take out an enemy without being noticed.

On Land and Sea

The navy has one vehicle that can tackle both the land and water. A hovercraft rides on a cushion of air. That means it can travel over almost any surface. The navy often uses hovercraft to move troops and equipment from a ship to land.

Submarines spend most of their time underwater.
They surface when coming to port or
for emergencies.

US Navy hospital ships helped provide medical care during the 2020 COVID-19 crisis. The navy also helps with search and rescue missions and assists after natural disasters.

US Navy attack submarines are nuclear powered. They can stay underwater for long periods of time. Space for the crew is small. It takes special training to work on a submarine. Sailors take mental and physical tests to make sure they can handle the tough conditions.

Other Ships

The navy has dozens of other types of ships. Most of these have special jobs. Dock landing ships deliver equipment to land. Transport docks bring troops to land. **Patrol** boats are small, speedy ships that guard the coast. There are even hospital ships to help sick and injured people.

Mechanics work to keep navy equipment such as catapults running smoothly.

The navy has many jobs to do. Each sailor plays a role. The navy's equipment and vehicles help them get the job done.

Sailor Chris Kellogg said of life on a Navy ship:

> Being underway week after week gets tedious and makes me homesick, but I also get to do and see things that I just don't see at home. On nice days, I go out on the open-air decks at the front and back of the ship . . . and watch dolphins play in the ship's **wake**.

Source: Chris Kellogg. "A Day in the Life of a Sailor." *Navy Live*, 25 July 2014, navylive.dodlive.mil. Accessed 24 Mar. 2020.

What's the Big Idea?

What is this quote's main idea? Explain how the main idea is supported by details.

Tomahawk Missile

- Rocket-powered weapon

- Can fly for 1,000 miles (1,600 km) at 550 miles per hour (885 km/h)

- First used in 1991

Carrier
USS *Gerald R. Ford*

- One of the largest warships ever built
- Named after the thirty-eighth US president
- Nuclear powered

Submarine

- Nuclear powered
- Can stay underwater for a long time
- Crew requires special training

Glossary

arsenal
a supply of weapons

catapult
a device that propels an object forward

fleet
a group of ships under the same command

nuclear reactors
devices that produce power by splitting atoms

patrol
having to do with something used to guard a certain area

radar
a device that detects other objects in the area using radio waves

wake
the water a ship churns up behind it as it moves

Online Resources

To learn more about US Navy equipment and vehicles, visit our free resource websites below.

Visit **abdocorelibrary.com** or scan this QR code for free Common Core resources for teachers and students, including vetted activities, multimedia, and booklinks, for deeper subject comprehension.

Visit **abdobooklinks.com** or scan this QR code for free additional online weblinks for further learning. These links are routinely monitored and updated to provide the most current information available.

Learn More

Abdo, Kenny. *United States Navy*. Abdo Publishing, 2019.

London, Martha. *Military Ships*. Abdo Publishing, 2020.

Pagel-Hogan, Elizabeth. *US Special Operations Forces Equipment and Vehicles*. Abdo Publishing, 2022.

Index

About the Author

Douglas Hustad is a freelance author primarily of science and history books for young people. He, his wife, and their dogs live in the northern suburbs of San Diego, California.